To all my wonderful editors

A LETTER
FROM
PHOENIX FARM

by

Jane Yolen

photographs by

Jason Stemple

MEET THE AUTHOR

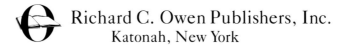

Richard C. Owen Publishers, Inc.
Katonah, New York

MEET THE AUTHOR

Text copyright © 1992 by Jane Yolen
Photographs copyright © 1992 by Jason Stemple

Richard C. Owen Publishers, Inc.
P.O. Box 585
Katonah, New York 10536

Library of Congress Cataloging-in-Publication Data

Yolen, Jane.
    A letter from Phoenix Farm / by Jane Yolen : photographs by Jason Stemple.
    p. cm. —(Meet the author)
    Summary: An autobiographical account of the prominent author Jane Yolen and how her daily life and writing process are interwoven.
    ISBN 978-1-878450-36-4 (hardcover)

    1. Yolen, Jane—Biography—Juvenile literature. 2. Authors, American—20th Century—Biography—Juvenile literature. 3. Children's literature—Authorship—Juvenile literature. [1. Yolen, Jane. 2. Authors, American.] I. Stemple, Jason, ill.   II. Title. III. Series: Meet the author (Katonah, N.Y.)

    PS3575.043Z473   1992

    813' .54—-dc20

    [B]   92-7795

First paperback printing   2016
ISBN   978-1-878450-34-0

Printed in Canada

9 8 7 6 5 4 3 2 1

For more information about our collection of Meet the Author books and other children's books visit our website at www.RCOwen.com or call 800-336-5588.

Dear Friends,
When we moved to our farm
in Western Massachusetts
over twenty years ago,
I wanted to call the place Fe-Fi-Fo-Farm.
But my wise and sensible husband David refused.
Our three children said
"Why not write a book about it, Mommy?"
so I did—*The Giants' Farm*—
which Tomie dePaola illustrated.
We called our house Phoenix Farm instead.

My house is not only a home.
It is my office as well.
On the third floor, in the attic,
I have two big work rooms.
One is my writing room where I start my day
early in the morning, about six o'clock,
still in my nightgown, a cup of tea by my side.
I can hear the bell on the nearby church
tolling the hours.

The other room, which used to be the maid's room
way back in 1896 when our farmhouse was built,
is my editing room.
Here I work helping other people
turn their stories into books.
I am on the phone a lot of the time.

Around ten o'clock each morning
I go to the post office and pick up my mail.
I get letters from editors
and letters from agents
and letters from librarians
and letters from movie companies.
But best of all I get letters from children
who have read my books.
I answer every one.

I used to go to schools
and give presentations to the students
but now I am so busy,
I only do occasional storytelling and readings
at places like the Holyoke Children's Museum.

Since I also write music,
I work part of the day at the piano.
I have done a number of music books,
some with my son Adam,
who is the *real* musician
of the family.

And I read, read, read,
whenever I can.

Sometimes one of my editors
comes to visit from New York City
or Boston or from San Diego
and stays overnight.
We work on books.

Here we are looking at the sheets of papers
on which a picture book is printed.

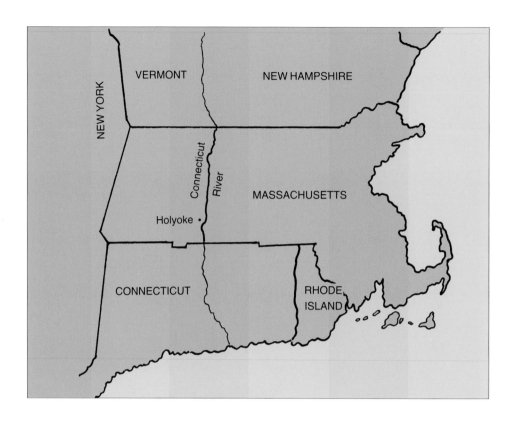

I try to walk every day that I am home.
My favorite walk takes me
by the Connecticut River.
When I am walking I often get ideas
for my books.
Sometimes a problem
that has been bothering me
about a plot or character
gets solved on these walks.

But sometimes I walk just for fun
with my husband or with friends.

In one of our barns
works a young man named Tim,
who prints t-shirts.
Often I go out to chat with him.
He has printed
special t-shirts for me.
Here we are working on the design
for a tour t-shirt
for a book tour illustrator Jane Dyer and I
went on in the Midwest.

I also lead workshop groups
for people who want to write
for children.
I have been leading the same group
at our town library
for the past eighteen years.
Many wonderful writers
have studied with me.

But mostly I write,
which takes a lot of thinking.
And thinking.
And thinking.
However, I have to admit
that sometimes I think best
when my fingers are
right on the typewriter keys.
Sometimes the stories seem
to leak right out of my fingertips.
At least it feels that way.

After I write a story
or a poem
or a picture book
or a novel
or a song
I give it to my husband to read
because he is my very best first reader.

I have published over 120 books.
Owl Moon won the Caldecott in 1988.
The Emperor and the Kite
was a Caldecott Honor Book.
The Devil's Arithmetic
won the Jewish Book Council Award.
Commander Toad in Space
won the Garden State Children's Book Award.
Piggins won both the Nebraska and
New York State Children's Book Awards.

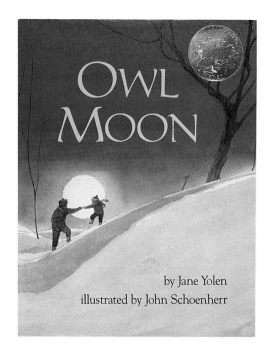

Oh, I have medals and medallions,
certificates and statues,
letters of commendation,
and seals of approval
from all kinds of groups.
But my best reward is when I hear
from the boys and girls who read my books.

People always ask
"Where do you get your ideas?"
The answer is—from everywhere.
From pictures and books and songs
and other stories and from
listening quietly to conversations.
Commander Toad came from a newspaper story
about a jumping frog contest.
Piggins began because I love British mysteries.
Sky Dogs started when I was reading
a wonderful collection
of Native American folk tales.
And *Owl Moon* is really the story
of my husband taking
our daughter Heidi out owling.

When our children were young,
David and I read to them all the time,
and not only at bedtime.
We read in the car, on camping trips,
and even when they were in the tub
taking baths.
We read whenever any of them said
"Tell me a story."
Now they are all grown up
and live far away.
Jason did the photographs for this book.
He has a degree in graphic design and business.
Adam plays guitar and keyboards in a band.
Heidi is a social worker.
She works as a probation officer
and lives with her three-legged dog in Florida.

When they all come home
for the winter holidays,
we have a great time together.
We sing. We tell stories.
And we always give each other books as presents.

If you ever come to Phoenix Farm
you will see my collection
of unicorns, selchies, wizards,
mermaids, and dragons.

Mostly dragons.
People keep giving them to me
because they know from my books
how much I enjoy them.
And I hope you enjoy them, too.
Your friend,

Jane Yolen

A Poem Written for You

A book can be a passport
To another time or place
Where dinosaurs still roam the earth
Or astronauts cross space.

A book can be a ticket
To a magic kind of realm
With unicorns or dragons
Or a Nemo at the helm.

A book can be a transfer
To another land or spot
Where people are a lot like us,
Or sometimes they are not.

A book can be a permit
To a world you've never seen
Where cabbages are big as malls;
Where all the suns are green.

A book can take you anywhere,
And you don't have to buy it.
Just borrow from the library
And snuggle down—and try it!

Other Books by Jane Yolen

All Those Secrets of the World; *Baby Bear's Bedtime Book*; *Bird Watch*; the *Commander Toad* books; *The Devil's Arithmetic*; *Dinosaur Dances*; *Dragon's Blood*; *The Emperor and the Kite*; *Encounter*; *The Giants' Farm*; *Hark, A Christmas Sampler*; *Piggins*; *Ring of Earth*; *Owl Moon*; *Sky Dogs*; *Sleeping Ugly*; *Street Rhymes from Around the World*; and many others.

About the Photographer

At the time Jason Stemple did the photographs for this book he was twenty-one years old and going to college in Colorado. He likes to ski, hike in the mountains with his dog Misty, listen to music, and take pictures. This is his first book.

Acknowledgments

Illustration on page 5 by Tomie dePaola reprinted by permission of White Bird, Inc. from *The Giants' Farm* by Jane Yolen, illustrations copyright © 1977 by Tomie dePaola. Illustrations on pages 24 and 27 by John Schoenherr reprinted by permission of Philomel Books from *Owl Moon* by Jane Yolen, illustrations copyright © 1987 by John Schoenherr.